Table Of Contents

Introduction

In the 1990s, the nascent internet was commonly referred to as the "information superhighway", a phrase that was coined by Senator Al Gore in 1978 according to most reports.

The funny thing is, even though it seems to be a very dated phrase to modern ears, it is still essentially true. The vast majority of people still use the internet as a source of information first and foremost, and this in itself should be no surprise.

Although this is open to debate, there is probably not a library or museum where there is more information available than there is on the internet, and of course, the internet has the vast advantage over every library and museum of being accessible at your fingertips - but there is no doubt that the nature of the internet is changing, and doing so at a pace that almost defies belief.

For example, while some brave and hardy souls had tried to publish video materials on the internet previously, it was really only with the advent of YouTube that video took off, and that is less than four years ago as I write (YouTube was launched in February 2005).

Yet video is now such an integral part of the everyday internet experience that it is hard to believe that there was a time BV (before video), a time when the internet was all about providing information only in written format accompanied by static images.

Another huge change that has become increasingly evident over the last 3 or 4 years is the boom in business that is being transacted solely through the medium of the internet. From massive monolithic global corporations like Google to people spending their evenings working away in their back bedroom, there are now millions of companies and individuals who are operating a business where they make money from the internet.

This is not new. There were companies making money on the internet back in the 'information superhighway' days, which helped to fuel the .com boom and subsequent implosion at the end of the 90s.

But what is new and different is the fact that anyone who has an internet connection and a computer can now start their own internet marketing business quickly, easily and with very little capital outlay.

Indeed, it is the latter fact that is one of the primary attractions of starting a business online, particularly in comparison to starting a 'real world' business where you would need offices, computers, telephones and staff. All of this is before you even start talking about investing money in inventory or stock, training costs and the like.

To start your own online business, all you need is a computer and a connection.

Well, actually, that's not strictly true…

You must bring something to the table...

While it is true that the only external resource that you need to start an online business is a computer and a connection, you must have some personal qualities as well, because without these them, it is going to be a lot more difficult to achieve success - not necessarily impossible, but definitely far more difficult.

The first thing that you have to bring to your business is an absolute determination to succeed. From the very beginning, you have to be completely, 100% determined that whatever you do is going to succeed, without exception. You have to be willing to do whatever it takes to achieve that success, even acknowledging that there will sometimes be a 'cost' involved (e.g. less time with your family in the early days).

You must also accept that there is work to be done.

If you have not already done so, when you start searching the net for information about starting your own business, you will find that there is a lot of nonsense flying about, and you have to learn to recognize it for what it is.

There is no secret, magic formula that is somehow going to mysteriously transform you from an individual who has no money in your bank account to one with a million dollars, in six months or less. That is called the lottery, not business, but you will undoubtedly see products that make outrageous claims of this nature.

These products are successful because everybody is looking for the secret shortcut to success that means they do not have to do any work.

Don't fall for this garbage. There is no secret, there is no magic formula

– success is in direct proportion to the amount of effort you put in, end of story.

You have to be organized and focused, and you have to have (and work to) a plan. If a job needs doing, then in the early days at least, it is down to you to get it done, and it won't get done if you are disorganized, lacking in focus or have no plan.

You have to be a little thick skinned too, because when you tell people that you are trying to earn money on the internet, many of them (none of whom have any idea what they are talking about) will mock

you and suggest that you are crazy. Ignore it, and bolster your spirits by remembering that it is you who will have the last laugh! The bottom line is, everything that you need to succeed in business in the 'bricks and mortar' real world is needed to succeed online as well, except for the cash to get your business up and running.

Understanding internet marketing

Most people come into online business or internet marketing with a vaguely held idea that they somehow want to earn money on the net. It is however necessary to have a slightly more developed idea of how internet marketing works and where the money is to be made, if you are to succeed.

Returning to our earlier concept, although it has changed beyond all recognition over the past decade, the internet is still primarily about providing information. Consequently, the basic idea behind internet marketing is that you start a business that can provide the kind of information people are looking for, and earn money in the process.

In its simplest form, this would involve nothing more than having an information product that people want to buy, and selling it to them. In the same way that your local storekeeper asks for money because you have asked them for a loaf of bread, you can set up an internet business where you sell information.

Alternatively, you can give information away for free, but do so in such a way that you earn money on the 'back end' from advertising. In this situation, you are not selling anything, but there is still money to be made (albeit generally less than you would make from selling).

However, it is extremely important to note that this is internet marketing we are talking about, with the key word being marketing. One of the greatest advantages of selling or promoting on the internet is that the net allows you to take your marketing message right into the heart of everyone's home, and allows you to do so at little or no cost.

Furthermore, because everything that happens on the internet is trackable and traceable, it is possible to target your promotional and marketing activities at exactly the people who best represent the potential market for your product or service in a way that no other advertising medium can.

For instance, if you were advertising Honda cars for sale on TV, you would air your advertisements during programs that appealed to the type of people whom your market research has indicated are most likely to buy a Honda. However, you would have little idea of how many of those potential Honda owners were watching the show, or how many who were watching the show decided to stay to watch your advert.

If however you are advertising Honda cars on the net, it would be extremely easy to make sure that your advertising materials were only shown to people who were looking for information about Hondas.

There is one other major difference as well. While you will pay in advance for advertising on TV with no idea how many people are going to see your advert, if you use paid advertising online, it is possible to pay only when people view your advert. Hence, advertising online is far more cost-effective as well.

When just starting your new business there is actually no need to start paying for advertising, because there are plenty of ways you can promote your business for free.

However, the important thing to understand is that the success or failure of your business rides on your grasping the central concept that everything is about marketing.

Your shop window on the internet is going to be a website, and many new online marketers make the mistake of believing that their website is the #1 'make or break' factor for their business. This is completely wrong.

You can have the ugliest website imaginable, and as long as that website is promoting or selling something that people really need or want, you will be successful. On the other hand, you might be the proud owner of the 'Mona Lisa' of websites, but if no-one is interested in your product or service, or (even worse) if no-one knows about it, then you will make no sales at all.

Your ability to market your business is the key to success, and there are two aspects to this marketing ability.

Firstly, you have to be offering a product or service that people want or need, and they have to want or need it enough to be willing to pay for it.

Secondly and more importantly, you have to do everything you can to get the message out about what it is you have to offer. If you do not do so, you could give away Learjets for free and you're never going to get rid them because people don't know that they are available.

Somewhere in the mix there, you have to have a website to promote your business, but it is far less important how pretty or technically advanced that site is. If the information that you are providing is what people need and they know where to find it (i.e. on your site), then you will be a success.

Taking stock so far...

Let me briefly summarize what we have so far, because from this point on, the focus and the tone of this book is going to change.

What we have considered up to this point is the theory of why you can make money online, and the theory of how you do so.

However, knowing every theory in the world is never to be any use to you if you do not know how to put it into practice, and it is for this reason that from here on, we are going to be strictly practical.

What I am going to do throughout the rest of this book is set out in detail how to launch one particular type of internet business.

So, the first thing to say is that this is not the only kind of internet business that you might start off with, because there are many different approaches to getting involved in the online marketing community for the first time.

Furthermore, while this particular business model has been extremely successful for millions of beginner online marketers (or 'newbies', as they are often referred to), the level of success that any particular individual enjoys will depend upon their own efforts and level of application.

From here on, I am going to focus on one business model that should see you earning money fairly quickly. Moreover, it is a business model where the amount of money that you earn should be in direct proportion to the effort that you choose to put into marketing it.

It is also a business that is easily scalable.

You can follow the step-by-step guidelines throughout the rest of this manual, set your business up for the first time, work on it until it is a success and effectively running itself on autopilot, before moving on to do the whole thing again.

In this way, from one simple business model, you can build a business empire that can realistically bring in thousands of dollars a month from a business that requires very little start-up capital (although once you are generating a reasonable incoming cash flow, you can invest some of that cash flow in tools and resources that will make the whole thing even easier and more profitable).

It has to be something that people need or want...

You are going to set up a business that supplies information to people, and in order to make money by supplying information, it has to be something that they need or want.

Note the order that those two words are presented in, need and want.

People are far more likely to be willing to pay for information that they really need than for information that they merely want. Hence, it is important to differentiate between the two different groups and their requirements.

A simple example will illustrate this point perfectly.

If someone keeps a dog as a pet and they want to train it to do tricks, or they want to learn how to groom it properly, then they probably fall into the category of people who have 'wants'. If, however, the dog incessantly howls throughout the night so that they never get a wink of sleep, they have a real 'need'. They might want to teach the dog to behave properly, but from their own point of view, they have a need to do so for their own health, welfare and sanity!

People who have genuine needs are the people most likely to spend money to try to find a solution to the problem that they have. Moreover, they are likely to be willing to continue to spend until they find that solution.

As an example, if someone suffers chronic back pain, they will buy products that give them information about how to get rid of their pain. If a particular product they buy does the trick, they will no longer keep buying products of this nature, but if it doesn't, they will.

Hence, the first step to setting up your business is finding the kind of things that people need and are searching for on the internet.

This is not to say that you cannot sell information that people want, because you can. However, it is far easier to sell information that people need, and in the early days, you want to make things as easy as possible.

Now, you may be wondering what kind of information you might supply to people, and how are you going to 'package' this information in a way that will make money for you.

The answer is simple. You aren't, because other people have already done the hard work for you.

People go online each and every day to find information about an almost unbelievably wide and diverse range of topics and subject matter. In effect, no matter what kind of information is available, there are people looking for it, and although most of the time they want that information for free, it is good enough, then they might be willing to pay for it.

Consequently, in most areas where the net is a popular information search tool, there are lots of products available for sale already. However, almost none of these products is doing anything more than scratching the surface of their intended target market.

As a result, there are thousands of companies and individuals who are willing to pay other would-be online entrepreneurs commission to promote their products or services, which is where you come in.

You do not have to source the information that you're going to supply to your prospects. You do not have to worry about spending countless hours researching your subject, weeks compiling the results of your research into a product, or building a fancy website.

You just need to find a suitable market to promote into, and then find a product that matches the requirements of that market.

This is the first practical lesson.

You must always establish that there is a demand for any product that you are either going to promote on behalf of someone else, or even create yourself (a little further down the line) before you ever consider getting involved.

However, the majority of 'newbie' marketers do things completely the other way around. They find a product to promote or (far, far worse), they spend weeks or months creating their own product without first trying to establish whether there is a demand. Not surprisingly, most of the time this approach is a recipe for failure, and clearly it is therefore something you should never even contemplate doing.

You must always establish demand before finding or creating a suitable product – no exceptions – always!

You know that you need to establish demand, but you do not know what products other people have available that might satisfy that demand.

For this reason, in these early stages, you need to create a shortlist of perhaps half a dozen areas of demand in which it might be profitable to work if there are suitable products available. The next stage is to establish how you do this.

Your initial market research…

Before setting off on your market research journey, it might make sense to take stock of your own situation, and what you already know. By doing so, you might be surprised how easy it is to come up with some ideas about the kind of information that people need.

For example, we have already mentioned people with back pain. Extend this idea, and you come up with people who are suffering from arthritis, people looking for information about gout diets, people with irritable bowel syndrome and so on. None of these conditions is particularly life-threatening, but every one of them is a painful blight on the individual sufferer's life.

How about people who are suffering financial problems (debt is one of the few growth industries at the moment!)? Would a person whose house is just about to be taken from them qualify as someone who has a desperate need?

I think that you could safely say that they would qualify.

I am not for a moment suggesting that you 'prey' on these poor unfortunates – you should only work with what you're comfortable with, and you must be very confident that the information you provide to these people is of value and will help them.

All you are doing at this stage is listing down ideas, and if you are not personally comfortable with any idea you come up with, don't go with it. Ideas are not in short supply, so just keep researching until you find something with which you are comfortable.

The World's population is getting (much) fatter at an alarming rate. Do you think that people who are seriously overweight have a psychological or emotional pain caused by their seeming inability to do anything about solving their weight problem?

Once again, the answer can only be in the affirmative.

Think about people who have just separated from their partner. If you could provide them with information that helped them to get that person to come back to them (assuming that that is what they wanted), it is a foregone conclusion that it wouldn't be that difficult to find a hungry market.

What about people who don't have a partner but want one? Online dating is definitely a market where people who have a real need are to be found!

Do parents ever have problems with their teenage children? Of course they do – all the time! They need help, so here is another one to add to your list.

After you have brainstormed for a while, you will probably already have a list of potential markets to consider. Let's expand that list a little further by looking at some of the online resources that allow you to discover the kind of information that people are looking for.

Yahoo! Answers

Yahoo! Answers is the internet's #1 question and answer website, a place where any Yahoo! member can post a question about almost any topic under the sun and have that question answered by other Yahoo! members.

The site is completely free to use, and is available to any registered Yahoo! member. The quality of most of the answers that you will find on the site is questionable at best, but the important thing for you is that you can use this site to discover what kind of information people are looking for.

There are several different ways to use the site to establish the kind of things that people need to know. One option is to scroll a little way down the homepage and to switch the 'Answer Questions' window to show the most 'Popular' questions:

How do you extend and collect paces on the lunge line?
3 ☆ In <u>Horses</u> - Asked by <u>D L</u> - 1 hour ago

 How many people in the adoption section have gotten hate mail?
4 ☆ In <u>Adoption</u> - Asked by <u>Camira B</u> - 2 hours ago

 What are the democrats' views on Obama's stimulus plan?
3 ☆ In <u>Other - Politics & Government</u> - Asked by <u>damon1570</u> - 6 hours ago

 How has pop culture affect the Wrestling Industry?
9 ☆ In <u>Wrestling</u> - Asked by <u>[Truth Trials™] Fa`a Samoa</u> - 5 hours ago

 Does anyone else remember the Duggars when there were only 14 kids?
2 ☆ In <u>Parenting</u> - Asked by <u>Candace</u> - 3 hours ago

 How to stay on task while writing a book?
2 ☆ In <u>Books & Authors</u> - Asked by <u>pretty_little_gumdro...</u> - 3 hours ago

 According to evolutionary psychology, people have affairs in order to pass on their genes?
2 ☆ In <u>Psychology</u> - Asked by <u>CNL: Diavolo Blu</u> - 9 hours ago

 What are reasons to take a medicine that weakens your immune system?
2 ☆ In <u>Medicine</u> - Asked by <u>raptorivaz</u> - 7 hours ago

Alternatively, there is a list of categories down the left-hand side of the page, and there are several of these categories (and sub-categories) where an educated guess would indicate that people need information rather more than want it. An example would be the 'Health' category, but others such as 'Education' and 'Family & Relationships' can sometimes turn up some very interesting ideas:

✓ Education & References

✓ Entertainment & Music

✓ Environment

✓ Family & Relationships

✓ Food & Drink

✓ Games & Recreations

✓ Health

✓ Home & Garden

The 'Personal Finance' subcategory of the 'Business & Finance' category throws up quite a few questions that would give you an indication of the kind of information that people are desperately seeking:

Categories

→ All Categories

→ Business & Finance

• Advertising & Marketing
• Careers & Employment
• Corporations
• Credit
• Insurance
• Investing

» Personal Finance

• Renting & Real Estate
• Small Business
• Taxes
• Other - Business & Finance

Related links

→ About Yahoo! Answers
→ Knowledge Partners
→ Forum
→ Blog

 I added a credit card # on pay pal, and did nothing else. Can I know go buy things on ebay?
☆ In Personal Finance - Asked by Brad D - 0 answers - 12 minutes ago

 Someone told to open a WELLS FARGO CHECKING ACCOUNT to send me money.?
☆ In Personal Finance - Asked by Moscowimb - 3 answers - 23 minutes ago

 Does anyone participate in online-surveys to get paid for working at home?
☆ In Personal Finance - Asked by A.C.Cobra - 3 answers - 23 minutes ago

 How to make money fast!? ?
☆ In Personal Finance - Asked by Jessica S - 6 answers - 32 minutes ago

 Im a member with 74 fishing what should i do to 99 fast and getting a good chunk of cash?
☆ In Personal Finance - Asked by Sean - 0 answers - 35 minutes ago

 Please help!! Where can I cash my paycheck!?
☆ In Personal Finance - Asked by anthony g - 4 answers - 42 minutes ago

 Can I still get the $7500 tax credit for the purchase of a mobile home with land?
☆ In Personal Finance - Asked by Jodi R - 2 answers - 43 minutes ago

 My Debit To Income Is 79% What Do I Do?
☆ In Personal Finance - Asked by kat a - 5 answers - 45 minutes ago

43 Things

43Things is a site where people list the things that they want to achieve, their objectives and desires. Consequently, it is another good site for discovering what members of the site need or want.

On the homepage, you will see the 'Need Inspiration' tag cloud, within which the entries that are largest and in bold are the most popular categories in which objectives are listed.

People are concerned about 'Money and wealth' (more so now than ever before), so you could dive straight into this particular category, or start with the 'Popular goals' link:

43Things is a site where people list the things that they want to achieve, their objectives and desires. Consequently, it is another good site for discovering what members of the site need or want.

On the homepage, you will see the 'Need Inspiration' tag cloud, within which the entries that are largest and in bold are the most popular categories in which objectives are listed.

People are concerned about 'Money and wealth' (more so now than ever before), so you could dive straight into this particular category, or start with the 'Popular goals' l

Need inspiration?

Popular goals Health Money and wealth School and education Work and career Family and home Friends and social life Travel Spirituality and beliefs Creativity and self-expression

Generally speaking, in order to obtain a generic overview before trying to narrow things down, I would use the 'Popular goals' link:

Creativity and self-expression

1. lose weight | Add to list
2. stop procrastinating | Add to list
3. write a book | Add to list
4. fall in love | Add to list
5. be happy | Add to list
6. get a tattoo | Add to list

'Lose weight' is always a popular subject, but I would imagine that very few people would think that 'stop procrastinating' would be such a major concern.

'Get a tattoo' might also be worth listing, because while it represents more of a 'want' than a 'need', it is still a massively popular topic. Wanting to 'Fall in love' and 'Be happy' would both be important features of a stable relationship, hinting that relationships are another pain area.

There are one or two extra topics from the 'Money and wealth' category that would be worth adding to the list as well:

1. save money | Add to list
2. get out of debt | Add to list
3. become financially independen
4. win the lottery | Add to list
5. pay off my student loans | Add
6. make money | Add to list
7. become a millionaire | Add to |
8. stick to a budget | Add to list

MySpace Groups

MySpace is one of the most popular social networking sites on the internet, a place where millions of individuals come together to discuss their interests, hobbies and desires. Within the site, many hundreds of like-minded people have got together to form Groups that focus on their particular area of interest, and so by investigating which groups are the most popular, you can once again get a fairly clear idea of the kind of information that is in demand:

Groups by Category

Activities (346875 groups)	Health, Wellness, Fitness (33329 groups)
Automotive (58841 groups)	Hobbies & Crafts (39619 groups)
Business & Entrepreneurs (29247 groups)	Literature & Arts (37284 groups)
Cities & Neighborhoods (45853 groups)	Money & Investing (17133 groups)
Companies / Co-workers (41517 groups)	Music (371821 groups)
Computers & Internet (20088 groups)	Nightlife & Clubs (71546 groups)
Countries & Regional (15241 groups)	Non-Profit & Philanthropic (25818 groups)
Cultures & Community (93240 groups)	Other (1478642 groups)
Entertainment (402962 groups)	Pets & Animals (43376 groups)
Family & Home (59836 groups)	Places & Travel (22845 groups)
Fan Clubs (280447 groups)	Professional Organizations (53763 groups)
Fashion & Style (90335 groups)	Recreation & Sports (155955 groups)
Film & Television (52578 groups)	Religion & Beliefs (124158 groups)
Food, Drink & Wine (46837 groups)	Schools & Alumni (205303 groups)
Games (85365 groups)	Science & History (11136 groups)
Gay, Lesbian & Bi (46073 groups)	Sorority/Fraternities (35031 groups)
Government & Politics (37688 groups)	

[Create a Group]

On the group's homepage, there is a comprehensive list of 'Groups by Category'.

By now, you should be getting a fairly good idea of the categories that you should be investigating to establish the kind of information people are looking for. However, there is one other consideration which I have not mentioned previously, and this is the fact that even some extremely popular categories are not really worth looking at, because there is no money to be made.

For example, while there are a huge number of MySpace 'Entertainment' groups, there is generally little or no money to be made in this particular area as far as online marketers are concerned. You will see how to assess this a little later, but take it from me that this is not a moneymaking category.

The money making categories to focus on are (once again) 'Health, Wellness, Fitness' as well as 'Business & Entrepreneurs', 'Computers & Internet', 'Money & Investing' as well as 'Pets & Animals'. All of these are categories where you will find needy people, as opposed to those in other categories who simply have 'wants'.

A little way down the 'Health' category groups list, you have people who have come together to focus on autism, natural cures and yoga. While the latter is probably more of a 'want', 'autism' is a definite need (particularly for parents of autistic children), and for those who are dedicated to living a natural lifestyle, using 'natural cures' is probably also a 'need' subject:

 **Autism Awareness** (Public Group)
Autism Awareness

 **Natural Cures** (Public Group)
Natural Cures
 Alternative
medicine, Natural living, through
healing herbs, sustainable living and
alternative medicine.

 **Vegetable Mafia** (Public Group)
For Vegetarians and Vegans to
network with one another.

 **Yoga Beatitude** (Public Group)
A positive place for true Yoginis and
Yogis everywhere.

Yahoo! Directory

The Yahoo! Directory is a listing of websites that have been submitted by their owners to Yahoo! for listing in that directory. The most important thing to understand about this directory is that a website that is submitted to it is not automatically accepted.

Websites are only accepted if they meet Yahoo! quality standards, meaning that the directory presents a snapshot of the highest quality sites on the net. Webmasters will only go to the trouble of creating a high-quality site if there is money to be made by doing so (almost all sites are monetized in some way), and that indicates a thriving market.

Choosing from the category listing on the left-hand side of the page, and again using the 'Health' category as an example:

Entertainment
Movies, TV Shows, Music, Humor...

Government
Elections, Military, Law, Taxes...

Health
Disease, Drugs, Fitness, Nutrition...

News & Media
Newspapers, Radio, Weather, Blogs...

By clicking on the main link, you will get a complete list of every health-related sub-category:

- Alternative Medicine (569)
- Chats and Forums (39)
- Children's Health (219)
- Conferences (15)
- Consumer Products and Services@
- Death and Dying@
- Dental Health (70)
- Disabilities@
- Diseases and Conditions (11205) NEW!
- Education (44)
- Emergency Services (516)
- Environmental Health (212)
- First Aid (26)

- Medicine (4495) NEW!
- Men's Health (55)
- Mental Health (769) NEW!
- Midwifery (41)
- News and Media (316) NEW!
- Nursing (380)
- Nutrition (427) NEW!
- Organizations (22)
- Pet Health@
- Pharmacy (1895) NEW!
- Procedures and Therapies (601)
- Professional Supplies and Services@
- Public Health and Safety (2434)

Look through those that interest you and you will again find many interesting subcategories that you had probably never thought of before.

Note that you are looking for sub-categories here – trying to compete in a broad, generic market at the levels we have been considering previously is not going to work, simply because the competition is too tough. For example, if you were trying to drive people to a 'Health' focused website, there are quite a lot of other web pages that feature this single word:

Results 1 - 10 of about 1,240,000,000 for health

Hence, you have to be looking for a small 'piece' or slice of the overall health market where you would have a reasonable chance of making an impression. Such a 'piece' of a large market is usually known as a market niche.

As examples, we have already seen that 'autism' and 'natural cures' represent subcategories of the health market.

It would make for more sense to investigate these in greater detail, rather than chasing a massive target that you have no chance of hitting.

Is there money being spent?

You should now have a list of potential ideas around which you could build your first online business. One of the final pieces of the research jigsaw is to establish whether it is worth doing so by checking whether there is any money being spent in any individual marketplace.

This is easy to do, and of course, costs nothing.

Take the phrase that is most appropriate to your subject (what is known in online marketing terms as a keyword or a keyword phrase) and run a standard Google search using that phrase. For example, if you want to know whether people are spending money on products or services that are related to autism, you would run a standard search using this phrase:

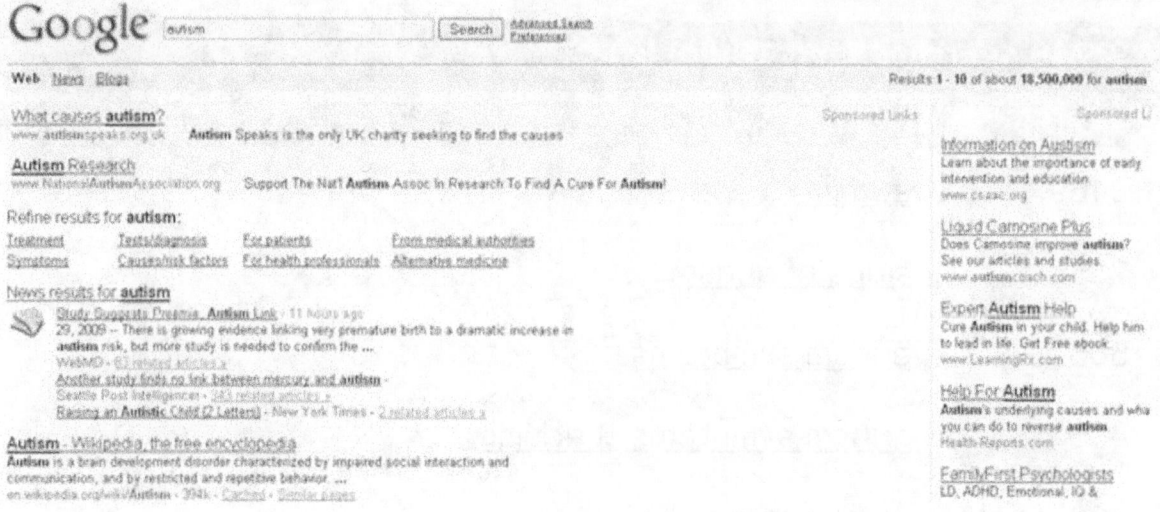

On the Google search results page, you see advertising that is placed there by Google. The more advertising there is, the more that would indicate that it is a mark it where there is money to be made, because otherwise, there would be no sense in companies or individuals spending money on advertising.

The most expensive adverts are those shown at the top left hand side of the screen, and there can never be more than three.

Down the right-hand side of the page, there can be a maximum of eight adverts. In this particular example, you don't have a perfect 'full house' because there are only two adverts at the top left hand side, but there are still nevertheless plenty of organizations and companies who are willing to spend money in this market. Once you have established that there is money in the market, there is one final thing that you need to confirm.

You need to know that should you choose to build a website based on this particular topic (autism), that there are enough people searching for information on the net to justify doing so.

Given that you have a list of potential site subject matter, if no-one were searching for the kind of information you are thinking of offering, you would move to the next potential subject on your list. However, assuming that there are enough people searching, the final thing to do is check the competition.

Can you attract visitors?

Checking whether there are enough people searching for information to justify building a site is extreme simple. Open up the free Word Tracker keyword research tool and type in your primary key word or phrase:

autism

9,948 searches (top 100 only)	
Searches	**Keyword**
3469	autism
755	signs of autism
565	autism symptoms
435	autism symptoms checklist
404	autism causes
381	autism research
322	characteristics for autism
170	jett travolta autism
161	physical characteristics of children with autism
156	autism home page
142	autism treatments

This indicates that there are just short of 10,000 people every day searching for autism related information on the net. 10,000 searches every day is a very healthy number, but you need to compare that to the number of web pages that are already presenting appropriate information:

Results 1 - 10 of about 18,500,000 for autism

10,000 searches a day becomes less impressive when there are already 18.5 million web pages indexed by Google that provide autism related information.

In effect, there is no way you can compete at this level, so what you need to do is establish whether there is a level at which you can compete.

Go back to the Word Tracker keyword chart and check each phrase in turn by running a standard Google search for each one. For example, this phrase enjoys 161 searches every day, which is a very reasonable number:

161   physical characteristics of children with autism

and by running a standard Google search, we can quickly established that there are only 184 web pages that feature this page:

Results **1** - **10** of about **184** for "physical characteristics of children with autism"

What you therefore have here is a term that is searched a reasonable number of times every day, but very few web pages that are presenting the appropriate information.

What this tells you is that if you use this particular phrase in your promotional materials and on your website, Google would very quickly find your webpage or your promotional materials, and as long as they liked your site, it should feature fairly high on the search results page.

Consequently, the next time someone is searching for information about the 'physical characteristics of children with autism', they would probably find your page featured in the search results and visit your site as a result.

I suggested that pulling visitors to your website is a crucial factor that will dictate how successful your business is. Finding low competition keyword phrases like this is one of the most effective ways of ensuring that you receive the site traffic you need in order to sell whatever product or service it is that you are promoting.

Run the same checking operation for every phrase produced by Word Tracker, and note down those where there are more than 20 people looking to information of the day, and less than 30,000 competing Web pages.

By now, we have established that there are plenty of people looking for information about autism, and there are search terms that you can use to drive visitors to your website. The final thing you need to do is confirm that there is a suitable product available that you can promote into the autism market.

Sourcing a suitable product…

Finding a suitable product could not be easier.

Visit Clickbank.com and sign up for a free account. Having done this, you can immediately promote any of the 10,000 products that are offered through the site, without further application or approval. Click the 'Marketplace' icon and type in the primary term that you want to look for and hit the 'Go' button:

Search the ClickBank Marketplace

Category: All Categories   Subcat: All Sub-Categories
Keywords: autism   Sort by: Popularity
Product Type: All Products   Language: All
Show: 10 results per page   Go   Reset

1) Yeast Free Cooking Manual/Cookbook. A Delicious Cookbook Full Of Great Cooking Tips, Easy, Yet Yumm Guide To Combat Autism, Candida, Fibromyalgia, Food Allergies, Arthritis, And The List Goes On!
$/sale: $15.49 | Future $: – | Total $/sale: $15.49 | %/sale: 58.0% | %refd: 63.0% | grav: 5.31
view pitch page | create hoplink

2) Essential Guide To Autism - * $18.67 Payout! 55% Commission! * New Upsell $48.80 Commission * Disc Check For Autistic Traits - Get What Really Works. *amazing Conversions* The Latest Affiliate Tools Here: to-autism.com/affiliate.html.
$/sale: $18.63 | Future $: $8.97 | Total $/sale: $24.36 | %/sale: 55.0% | %refd: 49.0% | grav: 3.93
view pitch page | create hoplink

3) Complete Autism Package. 1 In 166 Babies Have Autism. 75% Commission, Aff Tools W/dozens Of Article Copyrighter Spent 3 Weeks On Lp, Phd Interview With Autism Expert Trained By Famous Dr. Andrew Weil. A Autism…/affiliates.html.
$/sale: $25.79 | Future $: – | Total $/sale: $25.79 | %/sale: 75.0% | %refd: 16.0% | grav: 0.45
view pitch page | create hoplink

4) The Parenting Autism Resource Guide. You Get $16 Per Sale - 50% Commission. A Complete Resource Gu Diagnosed With Autism. For Affiliate Tools Go To www.parentingaspergers.com/affiliate.htm.
$/sale: $16.61 | Future $: – | Total $/sale: $16.61 | %/sale: 50.0% | %refd: 11.0% | grav: 0.27
view pitch page | create hoplink

This action will produce a list of all the products that have been called up by the keyword you have used. It is then simply a question of choosing the product that you want to promote.

If you are operating in a very competitive market, you will probably be offered dozens of different products to promote to your prospects. When this happens, you should try to select a product that does not as yet have such a level of popularity that it is already too well known in the marketplace. You would do this by checking on the 'grav' (gravity) figure underneath the product details to the far right as highlighted:
You are looking for a gravity figure of less than 100 points, so all of the autism related products shown in the screenshot are acceptable. You can see that the commission payable (to the far left of the green text line) varies, but do not be tempted to promote a product simply because of the commission payable.

Check the sales page of each product shown (from the 'view pitch page' link) to find the sales page that looks best to you. To a certain extent, choosing the best product from the sales page is a matter of instinct and gut reaction, so if you find one of the sales pitches stands out for you, use it because if you like it, it is likely that your prospects will as well.

Time for another quick summary.

You have found a market niche where there are plenty of people with a real need looking for information. You have established that there are low competition keyword phrases that you can use to drive visitors to your site, and you have found a suitable product to recommend to those visitors.

It is finally time to start building your site.

Keeping it simple...

There are many ways of building a website, some of which are far more difficult and complex than others. While at some point in the future you will want to move on from having a very basic site, that is the way you should start, because by doing so, you can keep the site creation process as simple as possible.

In this situation, simple means quick and that in turn means that you can channel your efforts into promoting your business, which as I

have already pointed out is the key to your success.

Here is what you do.

Visit Squidoo and sign up for a new account. Squidoo is a very simple, modular site building program that is a big favorite of Google. Using Squidoo, the mini-site that you are about to create is known as a 'lens'.

When you first log into your dashboard, you need to search for the button that will allow you to create a lens:

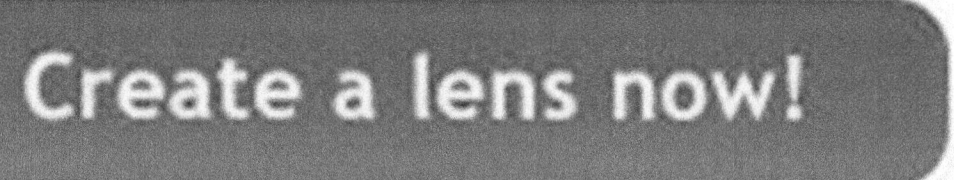

This action will bring you to the first step of the lens creation process.

The screen will look something like this. As this lens is going to focus on autism, that should be the

Step 1: What's your "lens" about?

A lens is just a fun word for a web page--a web page that focuses, like a camera lens, on a particular topic you're really interested in. People are making pages on everything from "How to Roast Your Own Coffee Beans" to "Why You Should Hire Me" to "Top 10 Wii Games for Kids" And LOTS more. What's your topic?

My lens is about:

Autism

Go to Step 2

just 3 easy steps to go!

On the next page, you want to do your own thing (it gives you a far greater degree of control) so check the appropriate choice and go to the next stage:

Step 2: What's your goal for your page?

It's easy to start a Squidoo page. It's not quite as easy to make it a masterpiece. But here's a great tip: As you build, think about what your goal for the page is. Are you trying to get the word out about an important issue? Market your business, or yourself? Earn some money for charity? Or just have fun organizing your interests? Get specific and tell a story, and we bet your lens will be awesome.

○ I want to get the word out about Autism (easiest option)

○ I'm gonna sell Autism stuff and earn $$, for me or for charity (money maker!)

○ I want to make a list of my favorite things about Autism (most popular)

◉ I just want to do my own thing.

Back

Go to Step 3

just 2 easy steps to go!

On this next page, you have to choose a title for your lens.

It will automatically use the 'my lens is about' information from the first page, but you should change this to reflect one of the primary keyword phrases that you found earlier using Word Tracker, in this case 'services for teenagers with autism'

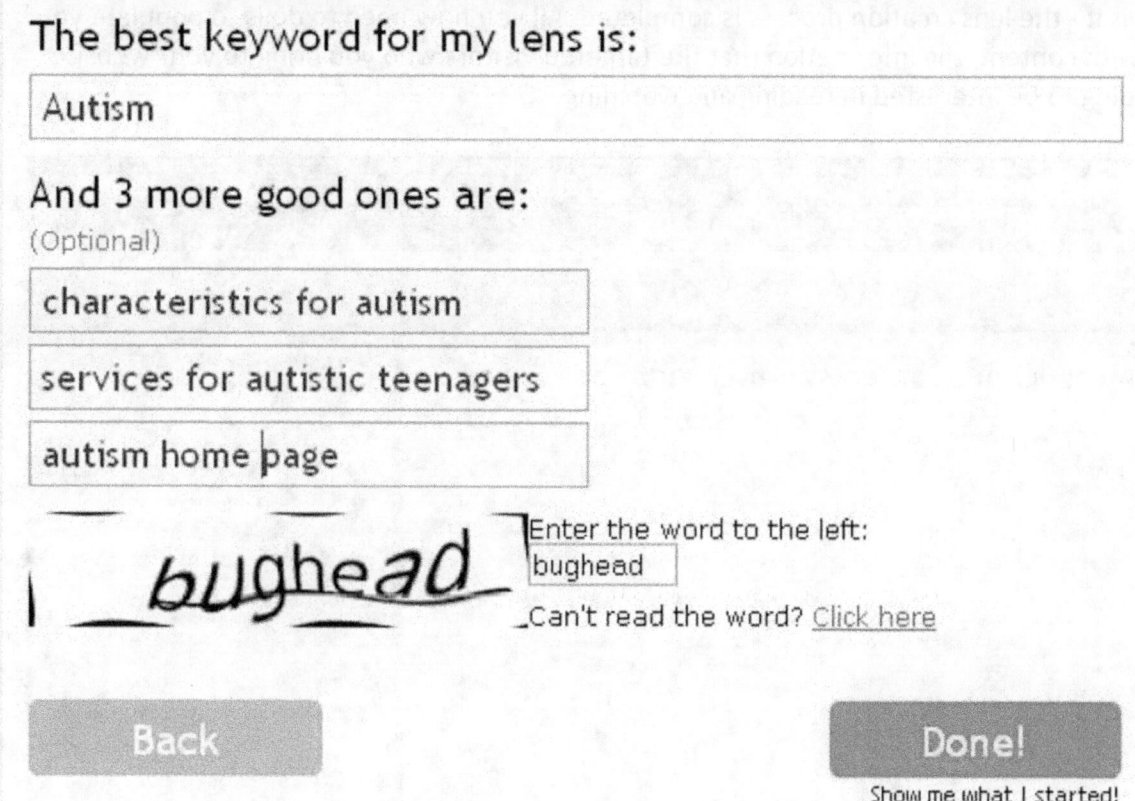

The best keyword for my lens is:

Autism

And 3 more good ones are:
(Optional)

characteristics for autism

services for autistic teenagers

autism home page

bughead

Enter the word to the left:
bughead

Can't read the word? Click here

Back   Done!

Show me what I started!

On the next page, including three more key phrases that are appropriate to your subject, insert the captcha code and that is the lens ready to go:

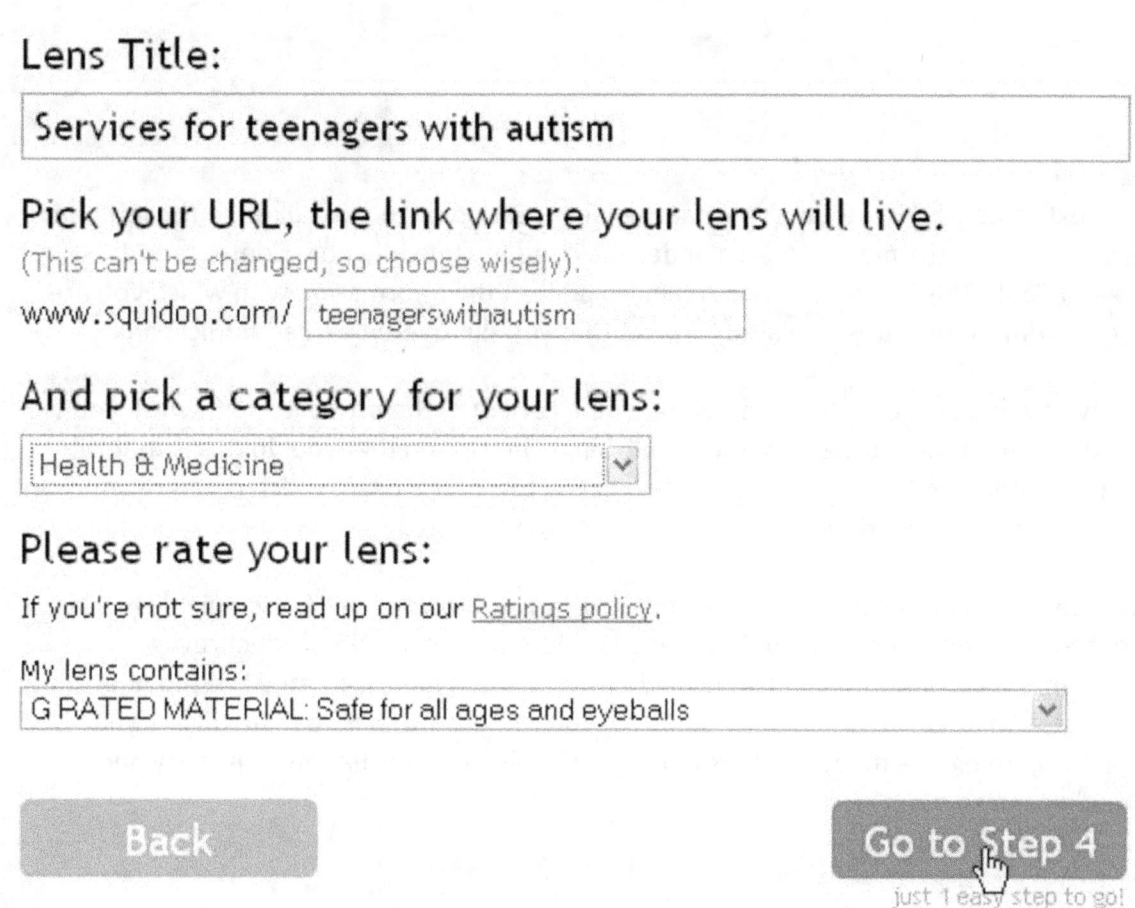

Lens Title:

Services for teenagers with autism

Pick your URL, the link where your lens will live.
(This can't be changed, so choose wisely).

www.squidoo.com/ teenagerswithautism

And pick a category for your lens:

Health & Medicine

Please rate your lens:

If you're not sure, read up on our Ratings policy.

My lens contains:
G RATED MATERIAL: Safe for all ages and eyeballs

Back   Go to Step 4

just 1 easy step to go!

That is it - the lens creation process is completed. All you now need to do is to populate your lens with content, the information that the targeted visitors who you bring to your website are going to be interested in reading and watching.

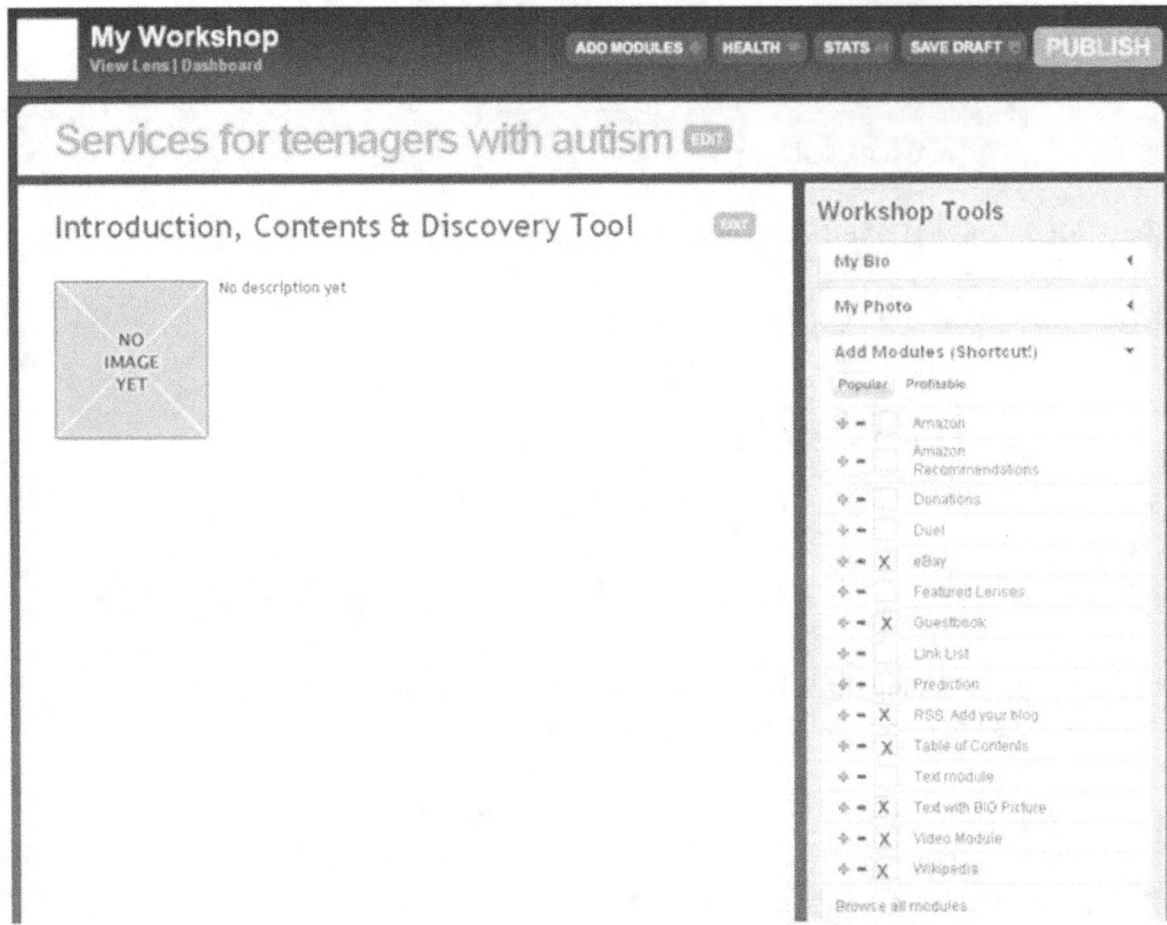

In the next screenshot, you can see what the lens creation page looks like. On the left hand side, you will note the main text area under the heading 'Introduction, Contents and Discovery Tool'. This is where you are going to publish the information with which you are going to promote the autism related product that you discovered earlier at Clickbank.

The way you you are going to do this is to write a review of the product itself, which you will then add to this area of the site before publishing. The reason that you do this is that this particular module of the site always appears at the top of the page, which is where you want your review to be every time a new visitor comes to your site.

Consequently, all of the other modules that you can add to your site (which highlighted in the right-hand side column) should be placed underneath this main product review:
In terms of the modules that you should add to your site, I have indicated the modules that I would use with a red check mark. By doing so, you can ensure that your site offers your visitors something of a multimedia experience, with video, information from eBay and Wikipedia, and so on.

Note that below the list of 'quick start' modules, there is a link to 'Browse all modules'. Take a look here as well, because there are many more modules that you can add to your site in order to make it more attractive and informative.

Because you have added a 'Guestbook' module, you are offering any visitor who comes to your site the opportunity of leaving their comments. The more comments you have, the more popular your lens will become within the Squidoo community, and that equates to more visitors.

In other words, you have built a site that targeted visitors will find interesting, and that is the key to making sure that they stick around, read what you have to say, and hopefully follow your link from the

product review to the sales page of the autism product you are promoting. When they do so, if they buy, you get paid.

You will also note that I have added the 'Text with BIG picture' module. This is something you should do (you can use the plain text module if you want) because having nothing more than your review on your site looks a little 'spammy' and unprofessional. If however you have additional text modules, this means that you can additional articles about your subject matter to your site, once again enhancing the experience of the visitor.

If you have the time, knowledge and inclination, it is best if you can write these articles yourself. However, there is nothing to stop you using other people's articles from a major article directory site like EzineArticles as your content materials.

Visit the site and search for articles about your chosen subject:

Find some articles that you would like to republish on your own site, and look for the 'Ezine Publisher' link to the right of the article title:

HOME::Health-and-Fitness/Autism

Are Psychosomatic Drugs Effective As an Autism Medical Treatment?
By Andrew Gowans

Article Word Count: 269 [View Summary] Comments (0)

Ads by Google

| toilet training autism | Autism Detoxification |
| inexpensive musical sensor is very successful with autistic children.. www.tinkletoons.com | Safe, Gentle for Kids Scientifically Proven Detox www.detoxamin.com |

Print This Article
EzinePublisher
Send To Friends
Add To Favorites
Post A Comment
Suggest Topic
Report Article

From here, you can download the article and then republish it on your lens in its entirety, including (most importantly) the original author details and link. You could do this with as many articles as you want, so this would be a very quick and easy way of populating your site with content if you don't have the time or the inclination to write your own materials.

If the only reason that you are not going to write your own materials is because you do not know the subject or topic particularly well, all you need to do is read a few EzineArticles articles and then rewrite them in your own words. The articles text is copyrighted, but the ideas and concepts behind them are not. From here, you can download the article and then republish it on your lens in its entirety, including (most importantly) the original author details and link. You could do this with as many articles as you want, so this would be a very quick and easy way of populating your site with content if you don't have the time or the inclination to write your own materials.

If the only reason that you are not going to write your own materials is because you do not know the subject or topic particularly well, all you need to do is read a few EzineArticles articles and then rewrite them in your own words. The articles text is copyrighted, but the ideas and concepts behind them are not.

Write your review…

Although it is possible that you would be able to write a more accurate and informative review if you were to buy a product that you are promoting yourself, it is not absolutely necessary to do so.

There are two ways that you can collect sufficient information to create your own review.

First, go through the Clickbank sales page and note down all of the major benefits. Remember that potential customers are only interested in what the product can do for them, so they want to know about benefits, not features. Generally speaking, you can usually find enough information on the sales page to write a reasonably good product review without doing anything else.

However, you might also want to search to see whether anybody else has already written a review, because that will make your job considerably easier. You do this by searching Google for 'product name + review' (or 'reviews'), so if you are promoting a product called ABC123, your search would be for 'ABC123 review'.

Between the sales page and other people's reviews, you should have enough materials to write your own. Don't make your review too gushingly complimentary about the product – add a couple of negatives to make the review appear more objective and unbiased.

However, in the final analysis, you should recommend it. When you do, make sure that you include a clear call to action (i.e. at the end of the review article, make sure that you tell your visitor that the product is highly recommended and that they must get their own copy), and tell them to click your link which must also be included.
Incidentally, you should not make it too obvious that your link goes to a product that you are promoting as an affiliate – something as innocuous as this would work far more effectively:

Introduction, Contents & Discovery Tool

ADHD & ADD - The Same or Different?

What, if anything, separates ADHD (Attention Deficit Hyperactive Disorder) and Attention Deficit Disorder or ADD?

Well, the two conditions do share many common features that would make them almost indistinguishable for most people in most situations. And both could generally be 'lumped together' under the catch-all term of ADD, too!

For example, the roots of both conditions are physiological, and both will demonstrate a multitude of 'symptoms' that are part and parcel of the respective conditions.

However, where the two conditions could be said to differ is in the following:

The major indication of ADHD is a clearly noticeable level of hyperactivity and impulsiveness. These are the indications that would tend to be clearly evident to the observant bystander.

ADD stands for Attention Deficit Disorder and the major indication of the presence of ADD is a general lack of concentration, rather then a surfeit of activity or energy.

Article continues HERE

The HTML code that you would need to create a link like this (using a standard Clickbank style 'hoplink' which you should replace with your own) would be coded in this way:

```
<a href=" http://yourCBnickname.aut1sm.hop.clickbank.net/"><strong>HERE</s trong></a>
```

Copy and paste this code at the bottom of your review page, add content from EzineArticles to several text units, add a few videos and materials on eBay, and the site should be fully ready to go.

However, don't stop there.

Come back every couple of days and add a new article (preferably one that you have written yourself), use the RSS feed module to keep your lens regularly updated and generally keep the site growing.

Google in particular loves Squidoo lenses, especially those where there is a regular supply of fresh, new (and ideally unique) content that you add, so keep Google happy and they will send traffic to your site.

However, this is not enough traffic to make your business successful.

Consequently, traffic is the next (and perhaps most important) aspect of building your business.

It all comes down to visitors…

There are lots of different ways that you can send visitors to your webpage. Should you choose to use them, some of these strategies involve spending money (paid advertising in other words), and others would be free in monetary terms (they cost you time instead).

While using paid advertising is undoubtedly the quickest way of bringing visitors to your site, it can also work out to be an extremely expensive business. For this reason, I would strongly recommend that at this stage, you use only free advertising and promotional resources.

At the same time, you need to start learning about the ins and outs of paid advertising.

I would therefore recommend that you try to find a free copy of the excellent AdWords guide published by a leading online marketing expert, Brad Callen.

At the time of writing, you could download a copy here or here, but if it is not available by the time you read this, try searching for 'Google AdWords made easy'. This is another good free AdWords guide as well.

Results 1 - 10 of about 8,370 for "autism forums".

Learn about paid advertising, but in the meantime, let's start driving visitors to your Squidoo lens using only free promotional resources.

Before we do, there is one final thing to mention. The more effort you put into promoting your business, the more results (i.e. money) you will get out. Remembering that this is your business - be prepared to use every spare minute you have to promote it.

Find a forum…

Forums are websites where like-minded individuals come together to discuss, debate and generally shoot the breeze about their common interests. Consequently, no matter what market niche you are operating in, if you can find a forum or noticeboard site that is focused on the same thing your recently developed site is focused on, then you have immediately found a group of people who are interested in what you have to say.

The first and perhaps most effective way of finding forums in your niche is to search Google using a search term something like 'your subject + forum(s)'. The beauty of using this strategy is that because the Google search engine naturally sorts everything in order of popularity, you would know that any forum site that appeared in the number one Google slot is automatically the most popular forum in your niche.

Even if you think it unlikely that there will be a forum in your market niche, the chances are that there are many more than you imagine:

Just a simple Google search of this nature will turn up many sites where you can get involved with other people who are concerned about the problem around which you have just created your site:

Web

Autism Spectrum Disorders ⬆❌
Welcome to the Autism Spectrum Disorders forum. Join the conversation.
forums.about.com/ab-autism/start/?lgnF=y - 86k - Cached - Similar pages - 💬

Wrong Planet - Autism Community ⬆❌
8 Oct 2008 ... Online community and resource for those with Asperger's Syndrome.
www.wrongplanet.net/ - 66k - Cached - Similar pages - 💬

Autism Forums ⬆❌
Select list of online forums which discuss autism spectrum disorders and related issues.
www.researchautism.net/pages/autism/resources/forums - 20k - Cached - Similar pages - 💬

Aspies For Freedom ⬆❌
This site has **autism forums**, aspergers forums, autism chat room, articles and lots of information in the autism wiki. Anyone can join, and members of the ...
www.aspiesforfreedom.com/ - 42k - Cached - Similar pages - 💬

Autism Support Forums ⬆❌
7 Jan 2009 ... Autism Support discussions and forums. Get and give support regarding Autism.
www.mdjunction.com/forums/autism-discussions - 24k - Cached - Similar pages - 💬

Groups Discussing **autism forums** for parents | Yahoo! Groups ⬆❌
Topics frequently discussed: area health education center, **autism forums** for ..... Topics frequently discussed: age of autism, autism forums for parents.

Every member of any relevant forum or noticeboards site that you can find is a potential customer for your business, but do not be tempted to dive straight into the deep end. You should take your time breaking yourself into the forum gently, reading and learning from other people before getting involved.

Nevertheless, you should start to get involved as quickly as you can, because this is how you start building a status and reputation in your niche. At the same time however, understand that within any forum community, there are members who have little knowledge, and there are members who are experts.

If you would not classify yourself as an expert, take a little time watching what happens in the forum so that you can work out who the experts are.

Once you are confident of your knowledge and your ability, start to get actively involved. When people pose questions that you can answer, do so. When you have questions, comments or suggestions of your own, start your own thread, because this will elicit responses and reactions from other members.

Becoming an active participant in the forums has two advantages, one clear while the other is perhaps less so.

Many forum sites allow you to create what is called a signature file, which is a short text description of and/or advertisement for your business (but do not make it a blatant plug, because that will not be accepted by most forums).

If you can use a signature file (I would recommend that you check before joining any particular forum site), this allows you to attach a short 'info-ad' to every posting that you make on that forum. Your promotional message is in front of other forum members every time you participate.

Perhaps even more importantly, however, participating in a forum allows you to establish your expert status. The importance of this should not be underestimated. If people believe that you are an expert (however accurate that assessment may be), they will follow what you say, and act upon your advice. Remembering that other forum members are superbly well targeted prospects for your business, this is an ideal situation to put yourself in.

So, find as many forum sites in your own niche as you can (also check Big-boards.com and forum showcase), and pick no more than half a dozen which are active and will allow you to add a signature file, before beginning to get involved as soon as possible. It is unlikely that you will see any immediate benefits, but it is equally likely that it should not take very long before the results start to become apparent.

Social sites for traffic and links…

Over the past couple of years, social bookmarking sites have become amongst the most popular sites on the net. Growing out of the original idea that it would be helpful if people could store their bookmarks from their computer externally so that they could access them from anywhere, social bookmarking sites are now hugely popular and represent extremely active communities.

The idea behind the social bookmarking site is very simple. When you find some content – it does not matter what kind of content is - it could be a video, and article, a news story or whatever – that you think is worth reading, you bookmark it to the social site of which you are a member. However, when you add this bookmark, it is public, so that

other members of the site can see it. You also have the ability to recommend it to other site members whom you suspect will enjoy it, from past experience.

If someone you pass this information on to in this way does indeed enjoy the content, then they might pass it on to someone else, and so the link is passed round, and everyone who enjoys it will 'vote it up'.

If something you have published on your lens is of sufficient quality to become hugely popular, then it may well end up on the homepage of the site. If this is a leading social site, then you can expect to see a deluge of visitors thousands strong within 24-48 hours. Although this traffic is going to be temporary, if you can only retain a small proportion of votes visitors as 'regulars', you have just given your business a significant boost.

Even if you do not manage to land on the homepage in this way, every piece of content that you successfully add to a social bookmarking site will create a link from that site to yours.

This is extremely important, because Google pays a great deal of attention to links when they are trying to assess how valuable your site is for search engine ranking purposes. The more important your site appears to be (judged by links), the better the search engine ranking of your site will be.

The only disadvantage of promoting your lens by submitting it to the major social bookmarking sites is that it is a time-consuming and somewhat tedious task.

It makes sense to take advantage of the free social bookmarking submission service offered by OnlyWire, that will submit your site details to 27 of the major social bookmarking sites. All that you have to do is log in to OnlyWire every time you add new information to your lens so that you can send details of your new post every time you make one.

This may send direct visitors to your site or it may not. Even if it doesn't, however, it will be instrumental in ensuring that your lens will attain a high search results ranking, and that in itself guarantees additional traffic.

Become a video star…

There can be little doubt that the most popular and probably the most effective way of promoting your business on the internet at this moment in time is by using video. You make a short video movie, post it to the leading video network sites like YouTube, Google Video and so on.

After that, you do whatever is necessary to encourage people to watch your video, on the basis that after they have watched it, they will visit your website to discover more of what you have to say.

Of course, there are many steps in this chain of causation, and the whole thing can go wrong at any time. Let us therefore move through the process one step at a time.

The first thing you need in order to market using videos is a video. Creating this can be a simple or as difficult as you want it to be.

At the simplest end of the spectrum, do you have 8 or 10 digital images that are related to your market niche stored on your computer? If you do, then you have the basis of a video. If, on the other hand you don't, you can download the necessary images from a site like Stock XChng.

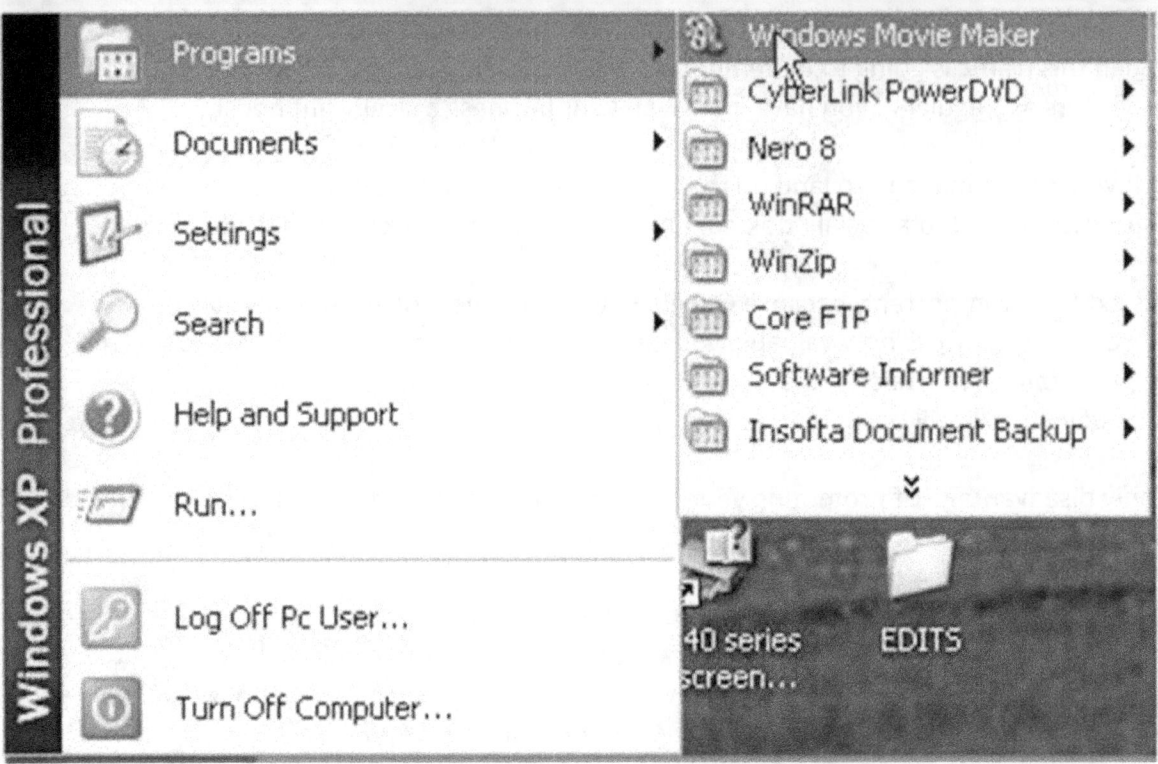

Next, open a free account with animoto.com, upload your images, add a soundtrack and upload the whole thing to YouTube. It is a job that should take no more than 30 minutes, start to finish.

Admittedly, it does not produce the most riveting video footage you will ever see, but it is extremely quick and easy to do, and if you want to get started with video marketing, this is as good a way as any to do so.

But while it is quick, using animoto is probably not the best way to market your business using videos. Firstly, because they are a montage of still images, they are not that engaging, and secondly, you can only upload animoto videos to YouTube and there are hundreds of video networking sites available.

If possible, it is far better to 'film' your own video materials, to edit them, and then upload the finished video to a selection of the most popular video networking sites.

Making a video to promote your business does not have to be expensive or difficult. Most digital cameras have a video utility nowadays, or alternatively, if you want to make a screen capture video, there is free software available at CamStudio.org.

In addition, the software that you need to edit your video is freely available too.

If you're using a Windows machine that uses XP or Vista, you already have Windows Movie Maker on your computer (in XP, click 'Start', then programs)

If you need to know how to use Movie Maker, try searching YouTube for 'movie maker tutorials', as there are plenty of videos that will show you exactly how to use the program. If you do not have movie maker, there is free editing software available over there

Once your video is ready to go, you need to add a title, description and tags before uploading to the network sites. Make sure that you include one or two of your primary keyword phrases in the title, and that you use keywords throughout the description as well.

Also, the first line of the description should be the URL of the page that you want the video viewer to visit after they have finished watching the video. Doing this ensures that there is a clickable hyperlink right next to the video and that there is a link from the video networking site back to yours. Given that Google loves links, this is extremely important to remember every time you upload a new video.

With the title, description and single word tags added to your video, it is time to upload it. As suggested, there are hundreds of video networking sites, but If you were to try to upload your video to every one of them, it would take you many hours of tedious work.

In terms of balancing time against effectiveness, it is far better and ultimately more profitable to upload your video to 10 to 20 of the most popular networking sites. There are a couple of sites that will help you to do this.

The first is TubeMogul from where you can load your video to most of the leading networking sites (including YouTube, Google video, Yahoo Video, daily motion and metacafé) completely free. The second site that you can use is HeySpread which is not particularly expensive to use.

Between the two sites, you can distribute your video to the majority of the leading video networking sites, giving your video maximum exposure for minimum effort.

Articles

Writing articles is a terrific way of generating a long-term flow of traffic to your site. It is also an easy way of promoting your business, and does not cost you anything.

The first thing that you need to do is write an article of 300 to 400 words, using a couple of keyword phrases from your list as the central 'core' of that article. Look for one keyword phrase that you would consider to be a primary keyword (i.e. one that Word Tracker indicates to be enjoying more than 30-40 searches a day) and one minor keyword phrase which only enjoys 10+ daily searches.

Use your primary keyword phrase in the title of your article and three or four times in the body text, with the secondary keyword phrase used once or twice as a maximum in the body text. Create a short summary of your article (two to three sentences is fine) and a list of keywords for that article.

Finally (and most importantly), write a short description or biography of what you do, focusing in particular on why anyone who reads your article should visit your site (because this article is going to be published externally).

In the description, include a couple of hyperlinks to your lens. The first of these hyperlinks can be the URL of the site, with the second link being the primary keyword phrase on which your article is focused. This is known as anchor text, and again, by using anchor text in this way, you're helping the search engines by telling them exactly what your article is about.

After you have created a suitable description, it is ready for uploading to half a dozen of the major article directory sites, places where people can go to read articles submitted by regular internet users about almost any topic under the sun.

Many article directories are extremely popular, with the ones listed below being arguably the most popular.

What is inarguable is that the most popular article directory is EzineArticles, and they will only publish unique article materials.

Consequently, after you have opened a free account with each of these directory sites, you should upload your article to EzineArticles first and wait until they have published it. Once they have done so, only then should you submit the article to the rest of the directories in this list:

http://ezinearticles.com/ http://www.articlecity.com/article_submission.shtml
http://www.ideamarketers.com/ http://www.articledashboard.com/
http://searchwarp.com/ http://goarticles.com/index.html

Incidentally, if you would like to know more about using articles to market your business, you can download a detailed free course about this particular promotional method (referred to as 'Bum Marketing') here.

It's persistence that counts…

All of the free traffic generation strategies highlighted in this section of the report work extremely well, and continue to work for many thousands of new marketers as you read this.

However, if you do not see a sudden deluge of visitors arriving on your site the very first day you launch (use Google analytics to check), do not be too dispirited or downhearted. It does not mean that you have failed or that you have done anything wrong, because in some market niches, the fact is that it simply takes time.

Persistence is the key to success. Even if you're not seeing the visitor numbers that you expected, keep creating new videos, writing new articles and never forget to submit details of what you have done to the social bookmarking sites every time you create any new materials.

The fact is, the more videos and articles you have published, the more traffic you will eventually see. If you keep contributing to the forums in your market, you will become better known, and people will begin to trust your knowledge and experience more and more every day.

Do not allow yourself to go into this wearing blinkers. You are not going to become a millionaire overnight, because building any business takes time, effort, determination and (yes, that word again) persistence.

Also, understand that this is not an exhaustive list of every free traffic generation method available. While using these strategies, you should therefore be on the lookout for other ways of promoting your business that will not cost you any money, because there are plenty of them out there.

Conclusion

Building a successful online business is within the grasp and capability of anyone, irrespective of their educational background, past business experience or even the amount of money they have available to sink into it.

However, building a business of this nature is a step-by-step process, and it is not one that you can hurry along. Everything needs to be done in a logical progressive manner, and as long as you follow what you have read in this manual in the order that the information has been presented to you, this is exactly what you will be doing.

Remember that it is all about finding a market where people need information, establishing that there is money in that market, and then finding a product that matches people's requirements.

After that, build a simple website that features your 'take' on the product you are promoting, and then finally, start sending as many visitors as you possibly can to that webpage.

All the time, keep reading, keep educating yourself and look for ways that you can improve your business.

However, do not allow yourself to be distracted by what you read. There are thousands of successful internet marketing entrepreneurs, and every one of them has their own view of what kind of business is the most profitable. It is therefore easy to get distracted, to race off to try another different type of business even before you have given the business that you have already established a decent chance to succeed.

Once you have set up your business as highlighted in this report, focus on it and do not allow yourself to be distracted. Have a plan that is related to this business only, and stick to it. Rather than charging off in a completely different business direction because someone has suggested that that is where the money is, focus all of your efforts on making sure that you keep improving your own business, because that is how you increase your income.

Keep all of this in the forefront of your mind, keep pushing more and more promotional materials out there into the marketplace, and you will achieve everything that you want to achieve.

As I suggested right at the beginning, there is no secret or magic key to online success. Follow what you read in this manual, put it into practice every day, and your new online business will be successful

www.ingramcontent.com/pod-product-compliance
Lightning Source LLC
Chambersburg PA
CBHW080525190526
45169CB00008B/3056